GOOD TO BE HERE
A BOOK OF MOMENTS

Sometimes I go about with pity for myself,
And all the while, great winds are carrying me across the sky.

Ojibway proverb

CONTENTS

Good Company

Mom

XII

✳

GOOD TO
BE HERE

THANK YOU

Mary	Sandy	Donna	Channing
Marion	Marsha	Mikey	Mara
Erick	John	Paulie	Connie
Sandi	Peggy	Clint & Co	Betsy
Alan	Pam	Chris	Sarah
Susan	Anne	Tom	Steve
Melissa	Helen	Jon	Angela
Vinny	Barb	Elizabeth	Bob
Leperas	Kathryn	Cathy	Keith
Nancy	Dottie	Blair	Shelia
Ellen	Raona	Edward	Jane
Judy	Val	Delaine	Cheryl
George	Benita	Randy	Deb
Jackie	Megan	Sally	Jeanne
David	Anita	Mary Ann	Shirley
Phil	Ruthann	Wally	Marcia
Georgia	Michael	Dale	Lillith
Norman	Joselle	Lynn	Regina
Joanie	Justine	Miriam	Kevin

...for your friendship, support, good advice and good humor.

❀

JUDITH
BARNES

"The only gift is a portion of thyself."
~ Emerson

INTRODUCTION

My father often said that every moment of every day,
each of us had a choice.

We could make that moment worse or we could make it better.

He always added he hoped I would make it better.
I usually try to do that, Dad.

The title of this book grew out of that way of looking at life.

The pieces in it were written over several years filled, at times, with darkness.

But those times were made bearable or transformed into
goodness by remembering that life affirming approach.
And the good times were made even better.

See Dad, I did listen.

ALIVE

My Own Child

So this is what it's like to be born.

A long, dark passage.
A blinding light.
So much pain.
Loud noises, confusion.

Ripped from the dark, I blink and shrink back.

I want the darkness again, the silence.
But instead, I slowly come alive.
I open my eyes, not sure where I am, even who I am.

Then I remember the crushing pain in my stomach,
the pre-dawn rush into surgery.

Later I learn a blockage had cut off the blood supply to my small intestine,
the result of a congenital condition I never knew I had. There had been two
surgeries, one to remove the blockage and an intestinal resection a day later.

Between the operations, I had been kept alive in a state
of suspension, my breathing done by a machine, my eyes
swollen shut from liters of fluid pumped into my body.

Shocked by the sight of me, fearful I would die
or suffer devastating physical consequences, my family was
frantic. But suspended in that darkness, I had been happy.

Maybe it was the drugs.
But I know it was also the cell-deep sense that I would live.

I came out of that darkness a new person.
I knew it the first time I stood up after the surgery.
I not only felt different, I was different.

The surgeon's report I read later said my intestines had been lifted out,
laid down outside my body and put back in several times.
Part of the intestines had also been removed.

But I didn't know that then.
All I knew was what I felt.
The core of my being had changed.

So I had been born again.
I even had a new navel.
The doctors had to slice through the old one.

I had become my own child, born out of my earlier self.
And when brought home weeks later, I was just like a newborn.

Freed from work and responsibilities for three months,
I slept, sat up, looked around, laid back down and slept again.

Then I walked, slowly and tentatively at first, not like the athlete I had been.

And then I started writing.

Not for work, for others.
For myself.
To develop my own voice.

Like a child, I was learning to speak.
And the pieces in this book were born.

5

❄

JUDITH
BARNES

GROWING UP

All Things Great and Swell

"Wouldn't it be great to get a cone tonight?" my Dad would say.

So we'd all pile into the car on a warm summer night.

Then as the sun faded and the stars came out,
we'd stand beneath the candy colored neon lights
of our favorite ice cream stand,
clutching our dripping cones.

"This is just great!" he'd say, licking the swirling, soft chocolate
ice cream round and round in a circle. My sister, mother and I all
followed his lead, licking our ice cream up to a little point.

It was great.
Lots of things about my Dad were great.

Great was one of his favorite words. So was swell.
And he used the two words often and interchangeably.
He loved to celebrate the greatness or swellness of a moment.

Like "That took a great deal of effort," he'd say after hours
of screeching sounds as I doggedly practiced a new piece
on my violin. "Great progress," he would add.

Or "This is a great day. Your mother and I are very proud of you."

He said that to me after I was awarded a doctorate one sunny May day.
Looking at the picture from twenty years ago – his beaming smile, his
arm around me, my diploma held up in his hand like a trophy – I can
still hear him exclaim, "Doctor Barnes! Doesn't that sound swell!"

Or "What a great country we live in!"

He said that often, especially during the noisy, colorful July Fourth parade he took us to each year in our hometown. As the soldiers marched by, his left hand would hold mine, his right hand would be over his heart and tears would be in his eyes. "A great country," he would murmur.

In the 1940s and '50s, his country grew to that greatness on the shoulders of workers like him. He showed up at the factory early, stayed late and for forty years was dedicated to hard work, good work and his company.

One summer in the '60s, as a college student desperately needing to make money for school, I worked on an assembly line in that factory.

It was hot, hard, dirty work.

Late one night on the line, when I could barely see through the sweat running down my face, a stooped older man with one arm came up to me and said quietly, "You Bob Barnes' daughter?" I replied that I was.

"Your Dad a great man," he said simply.
"He treat me like I the president of the company."

9

❀

JUDITH
BARNES

I looked up at him.

He was one of the night janitors, a black man in a city torn apart by race riots that terrified us all and brought out the prejudices of many. Using my father's favorite word, he showed me my Dad's greatest greatness.

My father died years ago.
But I always celebrate Father's Day by going out for a cone.

I look up into the darkening summer sky, lick the ice cream up into a point and say, "This is just great, Dad. And you sure were swell."

WHISPERING SCARS

I was twelve and badly wounded.
Slashed by sentences screamed at me and my sister.

"If I knew then what I know now I never would have had you!"

This from a mother who had become a monster, wild from surgeries that
spawned a horrific year of hormone storms, fast-moving fights, wounds.

Awful but unintentional wounds from someone who, but for that
crazy time, always told us how much she wanted us, loved us.

Those wounds became a part of me, though never all of me.

And wounds do talk.

They try to get attention, shouting I'm still here, help me, heal me, damn it!

They drink too much, eat too much, spend or work or play too much or have
too many bad encounters with ghastly descendents of the original aggressor.

Mine spoke through beautiful things bought to cover a lingering ugliness.

I had to teach myself to hear them.
Learn when not to listen. When to talk back.

I had to learn not to be consumed by them.

With time and work, the wounds became less vocal, less demanding.

Now even the scars have faded.
They speak only in a whisper.

Small voices that help me tend well the wounds of others.

SIT STILL

Finish business plan.
Start quarterly earnings release.
Release squirrel.
Get release signed for photo shoot.
Shoot TV commercial.
Watch TV program.
Program VCR.
Make up teaching program.
Buy makeup.
Sell garden books online.
Outline earnings call script.
Call about car.
Drive friend to memorial service.
Service heater.
Heat up leftovers.
Leave present for friend.
Finish presentation.
Start next presentation.
Start next writing assignment.
Start next press release.
Start next load of laundry.
Start next round of trustee calls.
Start next yoga class.
Start next thought.

Stop.

Sit still. Be still.

The words I hated to hear as a child, I now love to say to myself.

Once admonition. Now invitation.

❀

JUDITH
BARNES

VOICES

I was at lunch with a friend, listening to her read from a newspaper article.
She misread something, started the sentence, then stumbled over
the same words. It was no big deal. Just a small mispronunciation.

"There you go, screwing up again."

I tilted my head and looked at her.
She was talking to herself, and she wasn't joking.

"What's wrong?" she asked, suddenly aware I was frowning.

"I might ask you the same question," I said quietly.
"Are you hearing voices or are you being hard on yourself?"

"What do you mean?" she asked.
We looked at each other.

"The three of us should talk about it sometime," I said.
"You, your evil twin and me."

❀

That night at home, curled up in my favorite chair, I put down the book I'd
been reading and called her. When her answering machine came on, I told her
to give me a call. Then I made some tea and went back to read in my chair.

Suddenly I noticed the rain hitting my window.
It had become heavy, loud, almost ominous.

"Scary night," I thought to myself, as the wind howled.

I shivered and burrowed deeper under the soft wool throw.

The room, which moments before had seemed so cozy,
now felt cold, foreboding.

That voice, I realized with a start.

My own voice was scaring me.

The room hadn't changed at all.
Only my perception had changed.

"Cozy," I said, out loud this time.
"Warm and cozy," I repeated it like a mantra.

Though I had first been pretending, the room did seem more sheltering.
It felt warmer. I felt warmer.

I pushed the throw down on my lap, put my book on top of it and
looked out at the storm. Just moments before, it seemed to be raging
inside the room, even inside me, not just outside my window.

I thought about my friend.

She's genuinely happy and successful.
Good job, good marriage, great kids, many close friends.
But she listened to a dark and disembodied voice like I just had.

The phone rang.

When I heard her voice I said, "So the four of us need to talk...."

13

❋

JUDITH
BARNES

DANCING

"You're driving me to my death, I hope you realize that!"

Even as a thirteen year old, my sense of drama was highly developed.

I uttered this phrase through clenched teeth,
slumped and sulking in the back seat of the car
as my father drove me to ballroom dancing lessons
at Miss Enid Knapp Botsford's School of Dance.

I had gotten into the back seat because
my sense of symbolism was also highly developed.

I wanted my father to feel my distance, my displeasure.
That empty front passenger seat was, in my mind,
a dark message he couldn't fail to read.

My bad mood filled the car.

I hated everything about dancing class.

The frilly, girly dresses I had to wear did not, in any way, fit me...
a skinny, pale, awkward tomboy who always wore jeans and tee shirts.

The flowery headband that matched the dress couldn't subdue my frizzy hair,
which blew up into a kinky brown cloud from the dancing dampness
rising off the ballroom floor.

And the thought of a boy holding me close
and breathing all over me in nervous, shuddering puffs made me want to puke.

Especially when that boy was Charlie Brown.

That wasn't his real name.

But I secretly called him that because, like the cartoon character,
he had a big round head, a blocky body and was clumsy and awkward.

Worst of all, he had a crush on me, and he always asked me to dance.

His hands were damp and clammy.
The smell of his father's awful aftershave was suffocating.

And his girth, which brought him claustrophobically close to me
even when we were in that extended, stiff-armed formal dancing style,
made me want to lose consciousness and sink to the floor,
freed from all the torture.

The benefits of that torture didn't occur to me then.

But looking back, I realize life could have been like those awful, awkward
dances if not for another lesson I learned at Miss Botsford's.

Make something as good as it can be while you're doing it
and keep moving forward.

15

✸

JUDITH
BARNES

BIRD'S EYE

I love birds.

I love to watch them fly.
Swooping, soaring, gliding, wings out in a joyous arc.

I like to imagine all the different ways they see things.
From far away and up on high to down so low and close.

So at times I become a bird.

I spread my wings and fly away.
From people and places.
Noise and movement.
Deadlines, duties and dangers real or imagined.

I just fly away.

It may look like I'm sitting in my office
or my living room or right in front of you.

But I have flown to another place
and lost sight of all I left behind.

I see only sky and clouds,
feel the wind and hear its rush.

Then, freed from earthly concerns,
I fly back around and look down at where I was.

It all looks different because of the distance.

Perspective changes perception.

What loomed ominously over me when I was caught up in it
now looks smaller and less scary.

Or maybe truly monstrous.

It all changes.

Or I change.

The flight changes my sight.
New ways of seeing change my being.

I'm less caught up, less tied down.
Better able to judge size and seriousness.

Sometimes I misjudge conditions, my own or the elements.
I take off too soon, land too hard.

But the more I fly, the better I get.

And it all gets better, up there and down here.

17

❀

JUDITH
BARNES

Good Grief

I knew her well.
Lived with her forever.
Loved her even if I didn't always understand her.

Now she's gone, and I'm not sure how to go on without her.

The person I lost was me.
Or at least part of me, part of the person I had been for a long time.

The end of a twenty year relationship
ended the part of me that was part of a couple.

Though I knew for years the relationship with him had to end,
for the good of two caring people who had become so very different,
it still feels like a death at times.

The end was long in coming,
carefully examined and respectfully, even tenderly, handled.
So it is without the shock of a calamity.

And since we're on such good terms,
that end doesn't look like a death at all,
so the keening grief I sometimes feel seems oddly out of place
in our almost cozy, ongoing companionship.

The changes in me – and in him – are mostly inside each of us.

Nobody else really sees the difference.
Nobody else sees I'm mourning two losses.

Him and the old me.

But there are also reasons to celebrate.

It's spring, a time of growth in so many ways.

I'm relieved by the decision to separate after three years of hard work.
Grateful we've honored what we had by how we're taking leave.
Giddy, at times, from the freedom and the promises of the future.

So I am living two realities.

A sad requiem.
And an ode to joy.

Good grief indeed.

19

❀

**JUDITH
BARNES**

RESOLVE

I've always liked the word resolve.

As a noun, it means firm determination.

I looked it up in the dictionary decades ago.
Since then, I've tried to act with firm determination.
At fifty eight, I like to think I've succeeded more than I've failed.

But during some changes and challenges,
when firm determination was a bit elusive,
I started to wonder about the other meanings of resolve.

My musings came from a revelation as I was falling asleep one night.

When broken down into two parts,
the word resolve becomes re-solve.
Looking at the word that way suggested not firm determination,
but flexibility, looking at things from a new perspective.

Curious, I threw on my robe and walked,
in the dark, to my study.
I sat down at my desk, turned on the lamp,
and opened the dictionary.

A small pool of light fell on some meanings for resolve
that also shed some light on my future.

As a verb, resolve means to separate or distinguish things.
Decide on a course of action, find a solution.
Turn something at a distance into a different form when it's seen clearly.
Like my future?

It also means to cause a harmonic change and to heal.

That last definition of resolve got me thinking.
Maybe I needed to be a verb, not a noun.

Some very big changes – the peaceful
yet still painful end of a twenty year relationship,
the sad but exhilarating move from a longtime home,
the need to do different work – were making my future
and even my future identity disturbingly unclear.

But taking a new look at the word resolve helped show me how to go forward.

Sure, I could still act with firm determination.

But now I would be firm in my determination to remain flexible.
To see things clearly and from new perspectives.
To create harmonic change as I move towards a new future.

A new me.   21

My nocturnal revelation woke me up in more ways than one.   ❄

JUDITH
BARNES

DRESSED TO KILL

The black sheen of the jacket.
The line of the pants, straight down and slicing the air in a fast walk.
Shiny black shoes with glinting metal high heels.
Thick, twisted coils of silver around neck and wrist.
A flash of sparkling stones at the ear.

Looking at it all, you'd never guess it was battle dress.
Garment as armament.

All is fair in love and war.
And business.

Dressed to kill, I may have looked fierce, part of the advance guard
of young women on business fields of battle at the start of the seventies.

But my wardrobe embodied a confidence I didn't possess.
I was afraid and the tough look hid my fear, even from myself.

What I wore was camouflage as well as armor, and I needed both.

I fought hostility from some men, indifference from others.
Discomfort or distrust.
A dismissal of my abilities.
A disbelief that I was even there.
On their field, in their field.

I didn't blame them, really, at least not most of them.
They were no more trained to see me there than I was to be there.

Like any new recruit, I was clumsy, unsure, untested.
I didn't yet believe I could even do the job let alone lead others.

❄

And I sure was afraid of dying.

Not from blows to the body.
But from fear or embarrassment.
Those great blows to the spirit that can be just as deadly.

I knew the battle was a big one.
I was a foot soldier in a fight to change the world.

What better place to start than at the foot.

High heels leveled the field in a lot of ways
if I didn't mind being crippled from wearing them.

So I put on the heels.
The clothes.
The jewelry.
The attitude.

They helped me fashion my identity.

Thirty-five years later, I'm comfortable in my own skin.
What I wear now is adornment, not armament.

23

❀

JUDITH
BARNES

Rock On

At fifty eight, I became a rock drummer.
And why the hell not?

It happened last Sunday down in Woodstock.

I bought a drum.

A big, booming Ashiki.
A traditional African drum that rock drummers also play.
A drum of great beauty, with strong sounds, real power.

That rock and roll road trip to Woodstock started with a bang.
Actually, thousands and thousands of them.
At a heavy metal concert.
Where rock drummers wipe out the world of red wines and deadlines.

Forty years I've loved rock, rock drumming.
Gone to rock concerts since the '60s.
Went to this one for the grueling, dueling drum solo of Godsmack.

Primal, tribal thunder.

Two drummers in steely silver cages ensnaring black drums, blood red drums.
Tattooed arms wild and waving.
Sticks pounding, pounding, striking, slashing.
Flashing lights, deafening yells.
Thousands of arms thrust in the air in time with the moves of the drummers.

An ancient act of abandon.
Where sound beats back the mind so the force of the body is felt.

❋

Yeah, I was no businesswoman at that concert.

The drums resurrected young girl dreams.
Wrapped me in pleasure, possibilities.

Always have.
Always will.

I love to feel their fierce rhythms.
Because in my heart lives a being not so tamed.
The drums bring that wild one out.
Make me dance.
Keep me younger, stronger.

No rocking chair for me.
I'll rock out with my drum.

25

❀

**JUDITH
BARNES**

IN TIME

BUYING TIME

I was out driving on a sunny, cold afternoon.

It was the Friday after Thanksgiving, and I had planned to run errands,
do some shopping, catch up on some paperwork and
cross lots of things off my growing To Do list.

But, heading home, I had done none of the errands, none of the work,
no shopping and had crossed nothing off that list.

I had gone for a long drive instead.

Enjoying some leftover happiness from Thanksgiving,
I was in no hurry and on no schedule.

So while hordes of Black Friday shoppers filled the malls and the highways,
I drove alone down a long, empty country road,
listening to harp music and looking out on bare trees
and brown fields bronzed by the late afternoon sun.
The delicious smell of coffee filled the car,
floating up from the cup in a steamy swirl.

I was on a lovely road to nowhere.

The haze of pleasure continued as I got out of my car, humming.
I walked through the sunlit park to my apartment building and
climbed the stairs. I opened my door, walked down the hall,
stepped into my bedroom and stopped.

The whole room was filled with a deep golden light so intense I could feel it.

❋

**GOOD TO
BE HERE**

The late afternoon sun flooded in through the big south window
and spilled across the bed, the wood floor, and the creamy yellow walls.
The sky was a brilliant blue. On the big old oak tree outside my window,
a few red leaves moved in the breeze like small flickering fires.

It was all glorious.

I sat down on the bed to enjoy the moment.

Then I surrendered to the golden light and the laziness.

I kicked off my shoes, piled up the pillows and laid back against them.
I unfurled a soft woven throw and watched it float down to cover me.

I sighed.
A big, deep sigh that, like the sun, filled the room.

Lying on my bed, I was warmed by the throw, the sunlight and
the knowledge that the only thing I needed to do was…nothing.

What a luxury.

A simple, glorious gift that came from just buying myself a little time.

29

❀

JUDITH
BARNES

MAY I?

I graduated from college in May.
From graduate school the next May.
Was awarded a PhD twelve years later.
In May.

Met the man I would live with for twenty years on a bright May day.
After twenty years together, we agreed to separate.
Last May.

The lease on my new apartment started three weeks ago.
On the first day in May.

My new lease on life started after emergency surgery three years ago.
On the last day in May.

May.

The word means possibility.
Permission.
A wish or hope.

May also means spring sun.
Glorious greens and golds after the greys of winter.

New growth.

Especially today, a warm and sunny May morning,
as I stand in my new home looking out at a new view.

❀

FIRE CEREMONY

Snow is falling. Smoke is rising.
There's a blizzard outside, but the grill in the yard is fired up.

The glow of the fire is a cheerful orange light in the cold, dark night.
A taste of summer in the dead of winter.
Through the heavy, windblown snow I see him at the grill.

His head is down and his right hand on his hip while his left hand holds a
small brush loaded with his special sauce. Back and forth, back and forth
he brushes the sauce on the chicken in his slow, summer rhythm. There's
no hurry, no need to do it quickly so he can get back in the warm house.

He's happy at the grill, wrapped up in a heavy jacket and his thoughts.
It takes him back to his childhood.

He loved watching his Dad cook on the same grill out behind their house.
He savors all the memories of family cookouts in their back yard.

But standing at that grill now means his childhood is over.

His Dad gave him the grill when their house was sold and the family scattered:
mother and father moving south away from the snow; brother and his wife
and children moving and moving and moving again like chess pieces placed
by the unseen hand of a boss at company headquarters; him moving here.

I look out at him in the snow. I love to watch him when he's at the grill, cooking
up some magic, as he calls it. I know that means memories as well as food.

He deftly cleans up, closes the grill, touches it, then heads in, plowing
through the deep snow, the steaming plate of chicken held high in the air.

The fire ceremony is over.

31

❀

JUDITH
BARNES

Toes Up

It's a sunny Sunday afternoon in spring.

I'm lying on a blanket on top of a picnic table at the edge of a pond.
Over the tops of my toes, I'm watching ducks land in the water.

That's pretty much the only thing on my To Do list today and I'm doing it.

Flat on my back, toes in the air, hands under my head.
I'm watching the ducks land and the day go by.

It's a perfect toes up day.

Not a heads up weekday workday when I need to raise my sights,
stand up straight, face life and shoulder responsibility.

There's nothing like that about today.

Today I'm stretched out not stretched thin.
Flat on my back not flat out.

There's nothing wrong with all that vertical behavior.
At the right time and in the right place.
But I love being horizontal and seeing life from a different perspective.

Over my toes.

From that laid back position I don't see the big picture at all.
I see the small picture.

Like ducks landing.

❀

They slow the up and down motion of their wings
and curve them down into a half circle like a feathery parachute,
then lower their webbed feet, skim over the surface of the water and land.

Through lazy, half-closed eyes, I see two ducks come
into view, their wings curved down to land.

Three large fountains, their high plumes blowing in the breeze,
make windblown watery sounds as their far flung sprays
hit the surface of the water.

A child's voice squeals "Ducky!" off in the distance,
barely audible over the wind on the water, distant laughter
and the faint sound of an even more distant plane.

The joy of being active is balanced by the pleasure of being silent and still.
Laid back and lying down.

Toes up.

33

❊

JUDITH
BARNES

Night Wind

It's a winter night.
The wind chill is below zero outside. And inside.

I sleep with all the windows open in my bedroom.

The bedroom is on the top floor of a tall building high
on a wooded hill overlooking a river. Three large windows open
to the east, south and north so the air that blows up the river,
up the hill and then up the building, flows through the room.

I love this bedroom because of that fast moving night air.

It washes over me as I lie warm under layers of bedding.
It moves across my face and sweeps away the daytime,
leaving me light and floating through the night.

Since I was a child, I would let the night wind carry away each day.

So I don't lie awake with daytime troubles trapped in my mind or in the room,
like adult versions of childhood monsters lurking in the dark.
I send them away on the swift, dark stream of night air,
not to return because the current is too strong.

Especially tonight, when the howling winter wind blows up
wild waves of frigid air that break across the bed.

But bedding has been chosen for density as well as beauty
and layered for psychic protection as well as warmth.
So, snuggled deep under the covers, with only my face exposed
to the cold current, I feel safe and warm.

I take a deep breath, blow the day out into the night and close my eyes.

❂

Good To
Be Here

Ever After

I'm on vacation, dressed up for dinner and standing in the long,
elegant hallway of a gracious old Southern resort hotel.

Then I see them.

She is tiny, lovely, almost ethereal. In a black suit and pearls,
she is so delicate she should be wearing the filmy gown of a princess.

He is thin and pale but still looks strong, regal. His formal bearing contrasts
with thick white hair that falls boyishly over his forehead.

I stand by the columns of the grand dining room and
watch as they walk slowly toward me.

They're holding hands, leaning into each other and talking intently.

The early evening sun, setting behind the trees in the garden outside,
shines in through the row of tall arched windows and washes them with
a soft, golden light, making it look like they stepped out of a fairy tale.

But these lovers are in their eighties, something we don't see
in those tales of romantic forever after young love.

Never letting go of each other's hands, they walk down the hall,
wrapped up in the light, their conversation and each other.

I am unable to look at anything but them.

Happily ever after indeed.

A real fairy tale.

35

❋

JUDITH
BARNES

THINGS

FULL PLATE

I love my grandmother's china, now mine.

I look at its swirls and colors and I know
I've inherited much more from Nana than these dishes.

I have the same need to create and be surrounded by beauty.

Nana's real legacy to me?

Her artist's soul.
Her joy in transforming the ordinary into the extraordinary.

I see this in her beloved china.

Most patterns of her time were skeletal in their whiteness and stark simplicity.
But Nana's English china explodes with color and movement.

The glossy, cream-colored plate has fluted edges growing out of deep
ripples that start at its center. The surface is filled with a geometric frieze
that encircles dark vines, feathery fronds and blooms in deep reds, yellows,
blues and vibrant pinks. The plate seems full even when it's empty.

The pattern is Florence, named after the town in Italy renowned for its art.
And Nana was an artist.

Had she lived in a time when women were encouraged to develop
talents into professions, art would have been her calling, her work.
Instead, she channeled her tremendous creative energy into
transforming everything she touched into art, into beauty.

Even herself.

❊

In her seventies, living alone after my grandfather's death, she was still tall and slender. She would mow the lawn in lavender shorts, a faded ivory silk blouse knotted rakishly at the waist, hair tied up loosely in a pretty scarf and oversized sunglasses which gave her the air of a celebrity though that was not her intention.

She never dressed to stand out.
Being "showy" was her most severe condemnation.
She dressed to create and celebrate beauty.

She did the same with her home.

It was a rich, quirky kaleidoscope of styles and patterns and colors.
Fringed, circular red upholstered chairs were mixed with classic
Federal mahogany end tables. Here brass and crystal lamps; there
oriental carpets, Native American stone figures, Mexican woven straw
dining chairs. And at the center of it all, a scrolled, cream-colored
cast iron table with a glass top that sparkled under those plates.

Nana's place was magic to me. When I was young, I didn't realize how unusual it was in the cookie cutter conventionality of the 1950s. But I did realize her place didn't look like any of the other houses in the neighborhood.

Hers was exotic. She was exotic.

Her independence, her unique creative style was not the norm in the conformist, conservative decade of my childhood. But that simply didn't concern her. She quietly went her own way and, with an artist's eye and an easy self-acceptance, she created her own life as a beautiful feast.

The plates were a big part of that feast for Nana.
And for me, then and now.

❀

JUDITH
BARNES

Breaking the Fast

Damn, I'm hungry!

Buttery scrambled eggs are piled up on the plate
like a fluffy yellow cloud next to a thick slice of ham,
pinky red with small black grill marks.
Home fries, all crusty and curled, spill over the rest of the big oval plate.
Two browned and buttered English muffin halves sit
near the peak of the potatoes.

Steam rises up off the plate.

I close my eyes and inhale.
Now this is the life.

Outside the old country diner is a cold winter wind and an icy blue sky.

Inside I sit warm by the frosty window,
my hand wrapped around a mug of coffee.

The waitress puts down a big glass of orange juice,
then asks if I need anything else.

Nope, I answer, this is heaven.

I sit there, taking in the delicious smells.

My mouth waters.
My stomach starts to rumble, then gets louder, more demanding.

I hit the button for the nurse.

"I think things are working," I say to her.

"That was fast!" she responds. "I'll call your surgeon."

I lean back in bed and close my eyes.
I'm in the trauma ward of the hospital.

Tubes snake in and out of me everywhere.
For days I've had nothing to eat or drink except IV fluid.
Two emergency surgeries have saved my life.
But recovery depends on whether or how quickly
my taken-apart-and-put-back-together intestines
"get to work," as my doctor put it.

So I went out for breakfast…in my mind.
And my new guts responded.

Not mind over body, mind with body.

41

❈

JUDITH
BARNES

In Hot Water

"You're in hot water, young lady!"

When I was growing up, being in hot water was bad.
Not anymore.

Now it means I'm up to my ankles in the steamy hot water of a pedicure.

Eyes closed, head back, I'm sitting wrapped up in a soft robe
and the deeply padded comfort of the pedicure chair.

Cares and concerns flow down and out through the bottom of my feet,
disappearing in the swirling, scented hot water of the foot tub.

I summon only enough energy to curl my hand
around the chosen bottle of nail polish.

It's a rich, iridescent bronze, a fashionable interpretation of
dying leaves, I think, with the smug satisfaction of having made
a good small decision. When it replaces the summery pool blue
color I walked in wearing, I will be ready to step into fall.

Valerie lifts the bottle of polish out of my loosening grip
and begins her artistry while I drift off in a dreamy state,
wondering why more women don't die in the pedicure chair,
slipping off the seat and drowning in the bubbling water of the foot tub.

I fall into a trance undisturbed by the murmur of voices swirling around me.

I'm in that dense fog of pleasure that rises up when one foot is rubbed
with warm lotion and the other rests by a jet of bubbling hot water.

In this hazy, half-sleep state, a thought slowly comes to me.

Through time, washing a person's feet has been a sign of respect.

Some people might not extend this notion to a pedicure.
But it does make sense.

Because a pedicure isn't just about being pampered and polished.
Buffed, puffed and fluffed.

It's a way to honor all the things I do when I'm on my feet.

43

✻

JUDITH
BARNES

Easy Chair

It's late at night, the end of a long, lousy day.

A heavy snowfall obscures the buildings in the city and the wind
slaps me as I come around the corner and go up my front steps.

Home.

I shake off the snow and the day, go up to the bedroom and leave a pile of
problems on the floor with my clothes. Then, in bathrobe and slippers, I walk
back downstairs to the big landing on the second floor of the old house.

There it is.
My favorite chair.

A worn, dark brown velvet wing chair, it sits angled in the corner
of the landing. Resting against the back of the chair is a small
pillow my grandmother made out of an old oriental rug.
Her favorite woven throw lies across a footstool.

The wings of the chair reach out to me.
I sit down, put my feet up and lean my cheek against its wing.

A small pool of light falls on me from the lamp by the chair.
The rest of the landing fades into darkness.
So does a day filled with cold weather, cold people.

My cat jumps up and stretches out across my lap, purring.
I wish I could purr.
I sigh instead and sink into the chair, feet up and floating.

My chair has helped me learn that things are only as hard as I make them.
Life feels a little easier now.

❄

FEATHERS, NEST, NO EGG

I slow the car and stare.
Piled high by the side of the road is all this stuff.

Clothes, games, toys, furniture, kitchen things, bedroom things,
bathroom things and lots and lots of other things. In front of it all,
a cardboard sign is filled with scrawled red letters and urgency.

"FREE! TAKE IT ALL AWAY NOW!"

So many things their owners don't want anymore.
I drive by. I don't want them either.

Last year I moved out of the big, old house I'd lived in for twenty years,
so I had sold, given away, donated or thrown out a lot of my own things.

I had worked hard for them, enjoyed and dearly loved many.
But I had forgotten about others or tired of them, like a child
who eagerly rips open a pile of presents and then, satiated by the spectacle,
falls asleep clutching a favorite old stuffed animal.

What are the costs of all the piles of unwanted stuff at
garage sales, used clothing stores, vintage furniture places,
online auctions or by the side of the road?

Fancy feathers.
Overstuffed nests.
No nest egg.

And poorer in so many ways.

45

❉

JUDITH
BARNES

SOUNDINGS

No doors creaking as they're opened or closed.
No footsteps on the stairs.
No distant television noises, once a slightly annoying constant.
No snoring, once a bit more than slightly annoying.
No familiar house sounds or street sounds.

Nothing is as it was.

It's the first night in my new place.
After twenty years of living there with him, now I'm here.

Alone.

I enjoy solitude.
And I like silence as much as the sound of a friend's laugh,
a good conversation, even, at times, a snore.

But this is different.

❀

There's the dense and deafening emptiness of being alone in bed.
The strange sounds of new leaves rustling in the wind.
New nighttime building noises, new neighborhood noises.
Even my own breathing sounds different.

My initial impulse is to make noise, seek noise.

I want to turn on my favorite music, call a friend,
anything to fill this empty silence and surround myself with familiar sounds.

Over the days and nights to come, I know I will do some of that.

But I also want to stay still.
I want to settle into this new silence.
Listen to myself without distractions.

I came to this conclusion after I did something reassuringly familiar.

Surprised by how strongly I was reacting to the loss of old sounds and
the strangeness of new ones, I got up out of my new bed, found my
dictionary in its new place and read all the variations on the word sound.

There were the expected definitions about creating noise.
But what interested and comforted me were two others.

The first was about being healthy and secure, being sound.

The second was about testing the depth and quality of
water or other substances, about taking soundings.

I stared at those two definitions for a long time.

47

Then I put the dictionary on the table by my bed,
turned out the light and lay there in the quiet.

❀

So I could take soundings.
Of myself.

JUDITH
BARNES

Good Bye, Good Buy

I'm being sold on eBay.

Bits and pieces of me are sold, shipped and sitting
in buyers' houses all over the world.

Jewelry. Art. Books. Clothes. China. Flatware. Electronics. CDs. Even
the space-age silvery aluminum Christmas tree I hated when my parents
bought it back in 1960, now a big ticket nostalgia item for Baby Boomers.

What made me sell off pieces of myself?
A reaction to having been super-sized.

Living in a huge old house, I never had to throw anything out,
so things flew in the door and landed everywhere.
Four floors filled, attic to basement.

Twenty years of stuff, much of it lovely and even much loved.
Just too much of it.

Everywhere I looked there was stuff on top of, next to, under and even
stuffed into other stuff. The house was stuffed, its arteries clogged. Literally.

My resolution last New Year's Eve?
A cleansing diet.

I wanted to lose the weight of it all, for me and the house.
I wanted to remove the burden of having to care for it,
pay attention to it, bump into it, move around it or move it all around.

So I threw things out.
Gave things away.
Had a friend sell things on eBay.

❀

A childhood doll is now making a doll collector happy in the Midwest.
Funky earrings I bought in the '70s are now vintage, though that's tough
for me to accept, and they're being worn by retro fans in California.
Some of my garden books are in the hands of garden lovers
from England to New England. Jazz CDs I listened to over and over
are playing to new audiences around the country.

I'm flying off the shelf in the virtual store that's eBay,
and putting pieces of myself up for purchase has been pretty interesting.

Profitable? Sometimes.

The aluminum Christmas tree that cost $29 in 1960 sold for $325. But
some jewelry I paid a lot for just three years ago went for lots less than
I paid. However, money takes up less space than what it's replacing.

Fun? Surprisingly.

I thought it would be hard to sell my things but it became easier
when they were recycled then appreciated by others.
And I'm not selling beloved favorites or family treasures:
not even my mother, the one person who actually liked
that aluminum tree, would call it a family treasure.

Educational? Definitely.

It's been years since I used, thought of or even saw
some things I once thought I had to have. So as I shed them,
I'm shedding some illusions and learning more about who I am.

When I'm done, I'll see what's left of me.

49

❀

JUDITH
BARNES

HUMOR & SENSE

LIFE SUPPORT

"Bag must match shoes."

Though a fan of high fashion, I was referring to a colostomy bag.
And I was hooked up to a ventilator.

My eyes were swollen shut from liters of fluid
pumped into me between two intestinal surgeries.

My breathing was done by a machine.
I couldn't see and couldn't move except for one hand,
untied after my family and the nurse responded
to writing motions I had made.

So I wrote that line to the surgeon sitting by my bed
by visualizing the words, then making my hand form them with the pen.
Like in that art class I had taken as a child, where I had been
taught to draw by looking only at the object, not the paper.

I wrote fifteen legible pages front and back.
Random thoughts.
Requests for drugs.
Conversations with people in the room.
Scribbled pages numbered and saved by my family,
fearful they would be my last words.

The doctors were disbelieving, my surgeon stunned, I later learned,
by the exchange.

"A grunt here and there is what we get from someone in your
state, not punch lines," he said when we talked about it later.

I thought about that time last night.

Getting ready for bed, I glanced down at the long, pale scar
running half the length of my torso.

Pulling my bathrobe on – was my sudden chill from the night air or
the memory – I went to find the pages. Five years later and far away
from that surgical intensive care ward, I sat down to read them.

When I finished reading, I knew why I had made frantic writing moves
with my tied-down hand. Why, when the binding was taken off
and a pen put into that hand, I wrote and wrote and wrote.

For me, life support was not the machine that kept me breathing.
It was the contact with others that kept me strong.

And a fashion sense that wouldn't die.

✺

JUDITH
BARNES

Locks of Dread

"LOOK! It's a WITCH!!!"

Damn, sometimes I just have that effect on men, I thought.

"But I'm a GOOD witch!" I said, kneeling down in front of him.

OK, so he was only four years old. And I was dressed all in black,
though it was a hot and humid August afternoon.

But I wasn't wearing a spooky black gown with pointy sleeves
or a black hat or a mean expression, just black cut offs,
a black tank top and a look of concentration
because I was wondering where I had put my shopping list.

And we were in front of the supermarket
which is not where witches usually hang out,
I thought, as his flustered father stammered an apology.

"It's the hair," I said to the father, lifting my hands in an airy wave
before an evil little impulse made me turn the gesture into something
more sinister and I stabbed the air just to spook the kid.

My wild summer hair has drawn stares for decades.
I've learned to live with it, even love it.

On dry, winter days or tamed by technology – hair products and a hot flatiron
– it's just long and mostly dark with big streaks of white framing my face.
But in the summer, untouched by that flatiron and unpolished by heavy duty
silicone gels that could matte down field grass, it explodes off my head.

❀

It can get scary.
It can make little boys cry, "LOOK! It's a WITCH!"

When I was younger, I was obsessed with having smooth hair.
Back then I wouldn't have found it funny to be called a witch.

Now I think it's hilarious.

But it's more than that.

Now it's about being comfortable in my own skin.
And my hair.

I have a different attitude.
And that's the kind of magic a good witch can conjure up.

❀

JUDITH
BARNES

FIGHTING WORDS

I learned to swear on Seventh Avenue.
The heart of New York's great garment industry.
The fashion capital of the world.

The swearing capital of the world.

If you can't swear, you just can't work there.

Fashion swearing packs so many hurled invectives into a demonic diatribe
that you lose track of all the shocking words, stop noticing how
they've been distorted into all the different parts of speech
and are just stunned senseless by its sound and fury.

I am usually known for taking a calmer, more collaborative approach.

By inclination and training, I prefer discussion, mediation,
a fulsome exchange of ideas, an airing of differences that
leads to greater understanding if not to agreement.

But spraying a poisonous vapor of swear words can be so very satisfying.
And spitting out "What the FUCK?" can really help a girl make a point.

Invectives can be effective.

I was ten years old when I learned this.

After being repeatedly and defiantly disobedient, I was stunned
into submission by my mild-mannered father shouting in a voice
strangled by anger, "Damn it to HELL, Judy Anne!!!"

I never forgot the persuasive power of that well-timed, well-placed,
well-deserved curse. It was the only time I ever heard my father swear.

However, my grandfather - my Mom's father - was famous
for his toxic clouds of curses.

He was a short, stocky Englishman, a brilliant engineer
who had played rugby and served in the British Navy,
both breeding grounds for blue streak swearing.

I was in my late twenties when I really saw the genetic link
between my grandfather and me.

Driving my mother home after lunch, we narrowly avoided an
accident after being cut off by a pink Cadillac convertible driven by
a beefy bleached blond. Frightened and furious, I angrily punched
my car horn. She flipped me off, thrusting her hand up and stabbing
the air, her middle finger a dagger with its blood red tip.

Like a person possessed and speaking in tongues, I bellowed back a
foul barrage as the cars roared side-by-side down the interstate.

When it was over and the she-devil had sped off an exit ramp,
her hand still defiantly thrust into the air, my mother sat
wide-eyed and stunned, staring straight ahead.

"Well!" She exclaimed at last.
"You certainly inherited THAT from your grandfather!"

"Nature then nurture, Mom,"
I said to the woman who also loved a good curse.

❀

JUDITH
BARNES

A Good Cry

I've found a great exercise.

Crying.

It's quick and easy. It doesn't require complicated equipment, fancy clothes or an expensive gym membership. And it can be done almost anywhere, anytime.

While less of a full body workout than yoga, crying has the same benefits.

A good cry can flush out a bad mood, calm the spirit and increase flexibility, opening the mind as well as the tear ducts.

Crying is less aerobic than running, less strenuous than weight training. But a howling cry sure can build strength. And it can provide a hot and heavy-breathing workout, especially when accompanied by wild arm waving or the heaving and hurling of heavy objects.

Crying is also a lot like another good work out.

Sex.

After a good cry, I have a profound sense of well being. I can even experience a blissed out familiarity with my inner self. But only if I reflect on the meaning of it all and don't just roll over mindlessly to go to sleep.

So a sob session can be great for the soul as well as the body.

But it's hell on the looks.
Crying makes me puffy and blotchy, red-eyed and wild-haired.

I don't cry often, but after I do, I feel great even if I look gross.

In fact, the benefits of a good cry have made me an energetic evangelist.
I'm a convert to crying.

I see it as the next big self-help movement.
With editorials praising its potential.
Infomercials and seminars on how to do it.
Drugs to help us do it longer, better.
Crying style books.
Sobbing spas.
Workshops on couples crying.
Tee shirts with tearful sayings.
Reality shows like American Breakdown.
Magazines like Tear Jerks, Sob Sisters and more, so many more.
Talk shows where celebrities cry their hearts out.

Wait, that's already happening!

Then, of course, like all fads and fancies, the crying jag will fade.

But those of us who know the cleansing, strengthening effects
of a good cry will still schedule those sob sessions.

❀

JUDITH
BARNES

Go Away

A getaway can be relaxing.
A Go Away can be a life saver.

Literally.

It can save me from doing hard time for murder or at least a felonious assault.

A Go Away is my adult version of a kid's Time Out.

"Go away, Stan. This meeting is not productive because, how do I put this delicately, you're being such an ass! So go away and have some herbal tea."

Herbal tea is funny to tough guys like my client, Stan.
Guys who throw back coffee, beer or scotch.
It's so girly it perfumes being told to go away.

Stan sneers and shows me what I call his cobra face,
squinty-eyed and venomous.

"Reptilian response aside, Stan, you know what I always say, 'You only hurt the ones you love.' Go away, Stan. Don't make me hurt you."

I get a smirk and a hand gesture that, if I chose to litigate,
would have me owning his company. But the Go Away,
which lasted only a moment this time, worked again.

His mood, his thinking, and the meeting all improve.

I've been a consultant for over thirty five years.
My clients are usually high powered, high-ego, aggressive Type A guys.
Guys who love hand-to-hand corporate combat.
Two have been women but they fit the same profile.

Sometimes they just need to get some distance so they can get
perspective, think more clearly. That's when I tell them to go away.

But sometimes I need to get away from them.

"I'd rather chew off my arm than stay here with you, Ben,
so I'm going to do the Go Away.
When I get back, we'll all be in a happy place."

I say this to a colleague whose bad day is now making everyone else's day
really bad. I get up, walk out of the room, close the door then open the
door, walk back in and sit down. I get a laugh and a better outcome.

But there are also times when the person I need to get away from is myself.

"You go with your bad self," I say to my Evil Twin.

She's the one who gets worked up over nothing.
Who feels sorry for herself.
Who tries to talk me into buying another piece of jewelry.
Most of the time, she goes away, and no jewelry gets bought.

So when in doubt, just get out.
Go Away.

❀

JUDITH
BARNES

GOOD COMPANY

LUNCH DATE

I had lunch with an old friend yesterday.
He's been dead for years, but we got together just the same.

I took a glass of iced tea and a grilled cheese sandwich,
two of our favorite things, and went to sit across from him,
just like I had during the thirty years of lunches we had shared.

But now we meet at a cemetery not a restaurant.
And I talk more than he does.

I've never been much of a cemetery visitor or gravesite sitter.
I rarely even visit the grave of a friend or family member,
preferring to keep them alive in my thoughts. But I miss the regular
lunches that had created the rhythm and richness of our friendship.

So sometimes I take my lunch and sit near him on my beat-up old canoe
chair, which, just inches from the ground, is perfect for a graveside meal.

It was cold and damp yesterday when I put my chair down on the dead
grass, a late fall day with biting winds and fast moving dark clouds that
swept over the sun. And it was chilling to picture him, all of them, up
there during the icy winter storms soon to sweep over that frozen
ground. I shook off that image and stirred the sugar into my iced tea.

"You're sweet enough, darling," he always said when I asked for sugar. I smiled.

I was just twenty-one and in graduate school and he was a big
lawyer in town when I met him, sent to him for legal advice.
We were friends from the start but he was thirty years older, so
when the lunches started, people thought I was his mistress.

We laughed at that.
And, for thirty years, we went on with our friendship and our lunches.

Towards the end, I would feed him as he sat slumped over
in a nursing home chair, his once quick mind unable to follow
even a simple thought, his tailored suits and starched shirts
replaced by the robe he wore day after day.

I stirred my tea, remembering the last time I saw him.
His son had called to tell me death was near.
I should come to say goodbye to him.

I sat with his family by the side of his bed that day,
all of us sad and silent, looking down at his shrunken, almost spectral figure.

Then he stirred and startled us out of our mournful silence,
pointing at me and exclaiming in a booming courtroom voice
not heard from him in years.

"I have not had sex with this woman!
It's the one case I lost that I really regret!"

He gestured dramatically towards us, the last jury before him,
then looked up at me and said quietly,
"But we had the real thing, didn't we, darling?"

He sunk back into silence and died the next day.

But the friendship lives on.
And the lunches continue.

65

❀

JUDITH
BARNES

BOY FRIEND

"Can you put your hand on my ass so people won't think you're my mother?"

He got a howl of laughter from me instead.

He's in his late twenties, I'm in my late fifties and we're together
outside an arena with thousands of kids waiting to see a rock concert.

We've been friends and colleagues for almost ten years.
But that isn't what most people think when they see us together.

It's either "Your son is so wonderful."
To which I usually say, "Thank you, I'll tell his mother."
And get a puzzled look.

Or, "He's so hot! Are you sleeping with him?"
I'm tempted to say, "Not yet!"
Just to get a very different look.

But I don't.
I behave.
Most of the time.

I've had guys as close friends since I was in the first grade.
I've worked in fields dominated by men so they've
been colleagues and clients for decades.

I hang around with guys of all ages.
I hang around with women of all ages too.
But that doesn't cause the looks, the questions.

Like "So were you his mistress?"

"No but thanks for asking!" I say to a neighbor who slyly asks me this after
the death of a beloved longtime friend, a lawyer thirty years my senior.

Or "Who was that young man you were sitting with
at the college hockey game?"

A bank executive asks me this with a leer.
I reply with wide-eyed innocence, "My teaching assistant."
His face reddens.
"Score!" I think.

Or this from a woman I barely know, "I saw you at the airport
last night with a good looking younger man and I was going
to say hi but I wasn't sure you wanted to be seen."

What?

I just stare at her.
If I didn't want to be seen with somebody,
would I go to baggage claim in a busy airport?

"Business colleague," I finally say, adding we had just returned from
a business trip. "Pretty good reason to be in an airport together."

Or "I hear you have a new boyfriend!"
An acquaintance says this to me in a tone right out of a tabloid headline.

❋

JUDITH
BARNES

"Well, let's see," I reply, "Are you referring to a young hockey player,
a business colleague, my teaching assistant, a long dead trial lawyer,
one of the high tech coworkers I join for lunch, a fellow board member
I sometimes join for dinner or a CEO who has been a close friend for years?"

I ask her this with acidic irony in my voice.
Irony she apparently doesn't hear because she chirps, "Oh, the CEO!"

"Nope," I say. "Not a boyfriend."

"But I heard it from someone who knows!" she insists breathlessly.
"Knows more than I know?" I ask incredulously.

I give up.

What more people should know is there can be a space
between the words boy and friend!

❀

SMOKED

It was Friday evening.
I was getting ready to go out.

Sitting at my dressing table, I was looking in the mirror,
finishing my makeup, when I heard it.

A small rustle of cellophane.

That devil!
What was he up to now?

I decided to play coy.
I ignored him and went back to putting on eye shadow.

Then I saw him.

Cigar in his mouth, he headed for the living room, leaving behind
the unmistakable impression that he wanted me to follow.

So I did.

I walked down the hall, went around the corner and saw him.
He was in my favorite chair by the fireplace.

Cigar in his mouth, he sat there quietly.
And the look in his eyes said "stay home."

The offer was too good to refuse.

Because the cigar, still in its shiny wrapper, was at a jaunty angle
in the mouth of my orange tomcat.

69

❀

JUDITH
BARNES

SANCTUARY

I look into her eyes though she can't look back.

Blinded from being shot, with so much buckshot still in her body,
she wasn't supposed to last this long, get this strong.

Four feet tall, bigger than I'd ever imagined.
Dense feathers the colors of soft sunlight on fallen leaves.
Talons the size of my hand.
They grip thick knotted ropes strung from the sides
of her open air, wire-enclosed shelter.

This magnificent golden eagle is just inches away from me.
Mortals aren't often this close to a creature seen
as a soaring messenger of the gods.

She can't soar now but she's safe in this sanctuary.
So are two looming bald eagles in the next aviary.

Their yellow eyes narrow to slits and lock on mine with an unmoving
gaze that makes me shiver. The biggest one wheels around.

A tangled stump of broken bone and bent feathers is all that's left of one wing.
He had been hit by another winged thing. A plane.

There are hundreds and hundreds of birds here.
All of them hit or hurt by something so they can't fly or walk.

They couldn't survive if they weren't at this sanctuary,
cared for, befriended, by a man who is truly grounded.

❋

GOOD TO
BE HERE

When he was young and on a military base in a tropical country,
he was haunted by the sight of birds crammed into squalid cages to
be sold. He bought as many as he could, just to set them free.

Now injured birds are sent to him from everywhere.
He sets free the birds he can fix, shelters those he can't.

The fields of his family farm are now their nests.

I slowly walk the acres filled with aviaries. I stop by a low fence at
the edge of a marshy area filled with geese, ducks and swans. A small
duck limps towards me, one leg bent badly, one wing bent also.

He looks up at me with his sweet, funny face.
Quack.
His call is feeble, as small as he is.

I look down into that face.
Quack, quack, I answer softly.

Quack!

His response is stronger this time.
He cocks his head, still looking up at me.
He moves his wounded wing just a little.

I bend down, wanting to be closer to him.
But a sudden pain makes me straighten up.
I reach out for the fence support.

71

❀

JUDITH
BARNES

Just weeks out of the hospital after almost dying, I'm wounded myself.

The long scar from my breastbone down over my stomach is
still raw and red, the two emergency intestinal surgeries that
saved my life still recent enough to cause intense pain.

Weak and tired now and in pain, I close my eyes.
I lean on the fence, hands spread out for balance.
Breathing heavily, I wait for the pain to go away.
As it does, I open my eyes.

There is the duck, still looking up at me.

"Hi buddy," I say softly.

❀

**GOOD TO
BE HERE**

ROAD TRIP

We're on a road trip, and the years drop away with each mile.

Driving north on a bright, frigid, winter Friday morning, we feel like five
kids heading for a sleepover, not responsible women in our fifties.

We get together and get away like this two or three times a year for
quick trips that, over decades, have helped build our friendship.

All the organization it took to make this happen is now forgotten.

We eat a long, leisurely lunch.

Sunlight fills the window of the restaurant,
falling on us as we sit crowded together at the table,
sipping hot soup, swathed in sweaters, leaning back and laughing,
feeling like we have all the time in the world.

Walking with arms linked back to the car, the wind howls and we
howl, throwing our heads back in hilarity over a funny story.

We drive into town and stroll down the street, holding hot cups of coffee.
We wander around, window shop, then shop.
We try on things we never would, never should, and find the misfits hilarious.

But each of us does find one wonderful thing that, whenever we
wear it, will remind us of this afternoon's fun and our friendship.

Then shopping bags are thrown in the car and after a short
drive, everything is hauled out and up into the beautiful old
inn with its gleaming wood floors and inviting fireplaces.

73

❄

JUDITH
BARNES

Rooms are chosen, suitcases unpacked.
Clothes are changed, slippers put on, blankets brought out.
Streetlight replaces sunlight coming in the bay window of our room.

We catch up and settle down.
One naps. One knits. One reads. Two chat.
Then we're all just silent, happy to be away together.

But hunger gets us moving.

Makeup is touched up, clothes are thrown on.
We run down the street to a corner bistro.
One voice cuts through the now frigid black night air.

"One block, you said, but this is one long block. I'm freezing to death!"

We make it there alive.
The food is worth the walk.
So is our funny waiter.
After lingering over coffee, we run through the cold night.
Back to the inn and our pajamas.

Talk goes on and on, then lights go out.

Suddenly, there's sun coming in the windows and a tray filled
with cups of hot coffee and pastries is brought to the room
by the one who always brings morning coffee on our trips and
always calls out, "Once a waitress, always a waitress!"

More lazy talk over coffee starts another day of just being together.

✻

Good To
Be Here

Then it's Sunday.

Already? We moan.

We get dressed, packed and pile into the car to go for brunch, wondering
how the time went by so quickly yet feeling we've been away forever.

Then we drive back down the highway and split up,
heading for our own realities.

But the goodbye is more spirited than sad because the next road trip
was planned on this one. These trips connect us through time
and across the distances that separate us.

They are the joy rides of friendship.

❀

JUDITH
BARNES

Raising our Voices

Fifteen people, each at the end of a long day.

It's dark and cold outside. We sit pale and tired under the
unforgiving fluorescent lights of our classroom. Nothing ties us
together except being in the same room for the same reason.

To write.
To find our own voices.

We are in a class on the personal essay.
It's called Writing What You Know.

When we started class, we didn't know all that much.

We didn't know each other.
Didn't know as much about ourselves as we thought.
Didn't know how to write about ourselves but still interest others.

Individually, our voices were weak, wobbly.
Together, they made up a crazy chorus of discordant styles and sensibilities.

Now, after weeks, months, even years of classes, of baring souls
and sharing sometimes terrible secrets, of gaining
clarity and courage, we know a lot more.

About each other and ourselves.

I now have my own distinct voice.
Each of us does.
Voices made richer by listening to others.

❀

Good To
Be Here

An attitude in his writing makes a faint appearance in my own.
A reach she makes helps me take risks.
A rhythm heard in his work echoes through mine.

But it goes deeper than that.

Seeing through her eyes opens my own.
Feeling his broken heart breaks down a wall around mine.
Hearing a beautifully written, spirited cry of celebration lifts my own spirits.

The class raises the level of my writing, my hopes.
My friends in class raise my awareness.

We get stirred into one another in our weekly chorus of words,
led by one who brings out the best in each of us,
helping us raise our voices in so many ways.

It's a writing class, I say to people.
But that doesn't begin to tell the story.

77

❀

JUDITH
BARNES

OLD FRIENDS

I wrap my hands around the cup and breathe in
the fragrant steam from the coffee.

It's 7:30 on a cold, grey winter morning.

I lean my chair back and drink my coffee. On the wall above me is
an old clock with a little door that flies open at the start of each
hour so tiny, carved animals can dance to a tinkling melody.

Everything is old here, familiar and comfortable.

The small restaurant – just two rooms – is on the first floor of an old
building in a small city. The carpet is worn thin from all the hungry people
who have come and gone and sat at these tables through the years. The lights
hanging down from the high ceiling are tarnished but brightened by sprays
of green foil shamrocks cascading from each light, a tribute to the ethnic
heritage of the owners and today's celebration of St. Patrick's Day. There
are little nicks in the heavy restaurant china, the tops of the small square
tables are dented and the spoon on my saucer is dull from all the washings.

Even most of the people in the place are older.

The owners are a couple in their sixties. The cook is a woman who has
been making great food in city restaurants for forty years. Two grey-haired
nuns sit at a table in the center of the place, their whispers as soft as if they
were in their church around the corner. Three retired professors debate each
other at a table by the front window, their serious voices a funny contrast
to the wailed falsetto of oldies coming from the radio near the cash register.
And, sitting at three tables pushed together and set for ten, are four retired
guys, each is in his usual, favorite seat. The empty chairs between them
will soon be filled by other men, each sitting in his usual, favorite seat.

❀

GOOD TO
BE HERE

I'm sitting in my favorite seat across the room at two tables pushed together and set for seven. The guys call it the Girls Table, and there's a wrinkled plastic sign by the sugar bowl that says RESERVED in a curly, old-fashioned script.

I get here early so I can sit alone and watch everyone arrive.

I love seeing the place fill up, hearing each new voice added, breathing in the cooking smells. Watching and then being in the center of all the delicious small rituals of friendship as greetings are called out, backs slapped, jokes traded, news shared, coats hung up, coffee cups filled.

This is a sweet tradition, friends meeting for breakfast here on Fridays.

Now my friends start coming in.

Two swing through the door, shaking snowflakes off their hair and coats. One gets out of her car and waves at us. Another sweeps in and falls into her seat across from me, rushed from an already busy early morning. Voices swirl around, mixed with the food smells and the cold puffs of wintry air carried in on each new arrival. Finally the last two come as the clock strikes eight and the birds begin their song and dance.

For two decades, we've had Friday breakfasts here. Like the guys across the room and the other regulars, we're nourished by this tradition.

Season after season, year after year, wearing sandals and shorts, then snow gear, then summer dresses, then heavy sweaters, the seven of us have shown up at these breakfasts.

79

✳

JUDITH
BARNES

Children have been born, grown to adulthood, had their own children.
Marriages have begun and ended, some begun again.
Lives of husbands, parents and friends have ended.
Jobs have ended, begun, ended, begun.
Good work has been done, bad habits discussed.
Help has been given when asked for or when needed.
Laughter happens often, crying sometimes.

And always there are arms thrown across shoulders, pats on the
back and spontaneous hugs that adults don't get often enough.

All are plentiful here at this table, in this place filled with old friends.

80

❀

**GOOD TO
BE HERE**

DINNER FOR TWO

It is Thanksgiving evening.

Separated and living alone for the first time in over twenty years,
I sit at the table in the dining room of my new apartment.

Earlier in the day, despite our recent separation, he and I had
carried on our tradition and brought our families together to
celebrate Thanksgiving. It was wonderful family gathering but now
I am alone, eating warmed up leftovers from that dinner.

I look out my dining room window across the park circled by graceful
old brick buildings. Instead of the usual comforting glow of lights in
all the other windows, I see only a blurry, teary darkness. Many of my
neighbors are away, so the buildings are empty and dark, shadowed
in the cold moonlight by the stark branches of leafless trees.

Crying softly, I look down at my plate.
I say a prayer of thanksgiving for the meal, for the bonds he and I
would always have, for my family and friends, my good health and
good fortune and then I give thanks for my own good company.

The tears stop.
Surprised, I sit for a moment. Where had that thought come from?
Then I remember what an elderly friend of mine always loved
to say. "Darling, if you're not good company for yourself,
think what bad company you are for others."

It's a comforting, cheerful thought. I'm not alone. I am in my own good company.

More lights came on in windows around the park.
I lift my glass and toast my dinner companion. Me.
And I realize nobody ever has to eat alone.

❀

JUDITH
BARNES

MOM

84

✳

GOOD TO
BE HERE

To Have and To Hold

My mother and father married sixty five years ago and they're
still together, though he's been dead five years.

His ashes sit on the sideboard in the dining room. They're in a beautiful
cloisonne urn covered with enameled swirls of dark green vines, light green
tendrils and bouquets of small, delicate flowers in the warm and sunny
shades of summer, all outlined by the glinting gold of a fine, filigreed wire.

It's a cheerful urn that made my mother smile on the
cold, sad Saturday of his death that February.

It still makes her smile.

And it makes her laugh because my sister and I have draped over it a
silver decanter tag engraved with his name in elaborate swirling letters.

The presence of the urn also comforts her.

It makes her feel like she still has him, can still hold him,
which I have seen her do.

Now and then she'll give the urn a little hug or a small wave that, because of
her near total blindness, is just a waggling of her hand in his general direction.

When she has breakfast, Dad's urn sits in the sun coming through
the dining room window. At night, having him there pushes back the darkness
and makes her feel less lonely as she sets just one plate
on the table for dinner, not two.

She likes knowing that the cheerful flowered urn
will one day hold her ashes also.

So not even death will part them.

❀

JUDITH
BARNES

CHILD'S PLAY

It's a warm, sunny, spring Saturday afternoon.

I'm driving around town doing errands.
The window is down and my arm is resting on the car door in the sun.
My cell phone rings.

"Hi, Mom!" I sing out.

"Hello," she says in a dull, flat voice so different from her charming, chirpy lilt.
"What's wrong?" I ask quickly, trying not to sound alarmed.

But I am alarmed because she's frail, fighting cancer,
losing her sight and stubbornly living alone.

"I'm fine," she says in a weak little voice.
"Mom," I soften my voice, trying not to seem parental.
"You don't sound fine."

She sighs deeply, then tells a sad tale about how my sister's expensive dental
bridge had broken, the latest in a litany of dental woes for my sister.

"Is she home? Should I call her now?" I ask, relieved.
"Well, that would be very nice, Judy," she says sweetly.

Long pause.

"Because then she can say... April Fools!!!"
I laugh so hard I have to pull off the road into a parking lot.

"Every year you get me! Every year!" I gasp, when I can finally talk.

❀

GOOD TO
BE HERE

"Yes," she says proudly. "And, you know, I really had to work hard this year because I almost blew it yesterday when we were on the phone."

On that call, late Friday afternoon, she had talked about how the year was going by so quickly that Saturday would be the start of April.

"That means Saturday is April Fool's Day but there'll be no April Fooling Judy THIS year!" I had gloated. "No ma'am! You blew it! You won't sneak up on me tomorrow! I know April Fool's Day is your favorite holiday and you're the reigning queen but your reign is over now, honey!"

Apparently not.

Bested by her latest brilliant performance, I lean back in my seat while she smugly tells me how she had practiced speaking in a pitiful voice and had waited to spring her trap until late in the afternoon, when we had already spoken several times on the phone and she felt I had been lulled into an unsuspecting state.

I grin.

Despite all she has to endure now, she still loves to play.

87

❀

JUDITH
BARNES

GOING GRACEFULLY

I'm watching my mother leave, a little at a time.

She's almost ninety and nearly blind, with a cancer that pops up like some demented whack-a-mole game, forming lumps on her breast, then down below her ribs, then someplace else and someplace else after that and who knows what's going on or growing inside of her where we can't see it.

She's getting smaller and smaller right in front of me.
Moving toward the horizon.

She is ready to go.
But she wants to go gracefully.

She won't allow herself to be diminished by disease, blindness, age or loneliness. So her sense of perspective, her sense of humor and even her sense of style remain strong.

She dresses up every morning, though she doesn't often leave the house, and puts her earrings in by touch; has her hair done on Saturdays; listens to public radio every day and relishes talking about what's going on in the world; loves to reminisce about her first date with Dad and how handsome he looked when he came to her door. He died five years ago. She misses him, she always says, and is looking forward to being with him when she dies.

And she always tells my sister and me how we make her life worth living even if we were sometimes spoiled brats when we were young.

Were not, I always answer.

❀

I think about all of this as I drive home.

Then a car in front of me cuts off another car. A few miles down the road, I hear angry blasts from the horn of the car behind me when I slow down to let someone turn into the long line of traffic. A mile after that, an accident almost happens when aggressive drivers won't yield.

A lot of people do not go gracefully from anything.

On the final stretch home, under a white moon and on a highway mercifully free of cars and road rage, I reach the exit ramp.

The ramp is long and gently curved, built to slow the driver down and provide a gradual transition between two roads.

A graceful exit and a graceful entrance.

Like what Mom is trying to do.

89

✻

JUDITH
BARNES

MEMORIAL DAY

"Shouldn't you two be someplace?"
"Yes, Mom," I said.
"Right here with you."

I looked over at my sister, then down at Mom, sitting bent over
in her kitchen chair. She was weak from a fight with cancer,
shaken and scared from a wild, three day ride with death.

It was Memorial Day.
Three days ago, I was sure we would have buried her by Memorial Day.

When she hadn't answered our frequent and increasingly frantic phone calls,
my sister and I sped to her house and found her pale and incoherent,
slumped over in her bedroom chair, unable to straighten up or stand.
Later, in the hospital emergency room, she laid limp on the bed, mouth
open, eyes closed, her face waxen yellow against the white pillow.

So small, I remember thinking then, looking down and wondering
if she was dying or just disappearing. My sister and I stood like
giants over her, guarding her in that helpful, hostile place.

But, as dramatically as she had declined, she recovered and insisted
on going home though she was so fragile it frightened us.

So here we were on this hot, sunny Memorial Day, back in her kitchen
like nothing had happened though nothing would ever be the same.

Happy to be home, she breathed in the familiar smells and
caressed the arm of the kitchen chair. My sister and I, standing
over her, were sad, worried, frightened, protective, exhausted.

❀

GOOD TO
BE HERE

We stayed for hours, watching her make her wobbly way around
the house, sliding one gnarled hand along the furniture to get her
bearings and keep her balance while curling the other one around the
black cane we bought for her, which she pronounced very classy.

Finally, she said quietly and with some humor,
"Shouldn't you two be someplace?"

We had been dismissed.
She wanted to be alone in her own place.

My sister and I got ready to leave. We told her gently we
wished she had stayed in the hospital longer or gone to
rehab, which she also dismissed with an airy wave.

She stood at the back door as we walked down the curving driveway.
We looked back and called out, "We love you, Mom."
In a small voice, she said she loved us too.

My sister and I stopped by our cars at the end of the driveway.
We leaned against each other and cried, like when
we were little and something scared us.

Memorial Day indeed.

✻

JUDITH
BARNES

BIRTHDAY GIFTS

You're ninety today, Mom, and here's what you've been given.

Blindness.
Incontinence.
A long, jagged scab on your head from the latest fall.
Bruises everywhere from other falls as you lost your balance, your way.
Having the cancer spread to your brain, liver and lungs.
Being in a medical center not your sun-filled home.
Eating your birthday meal in a wheelchair, not your favorite restaurant.
Telling us you have decided it will be your last meal, your last cup of coffee.
We've had such fun, you sigh, sad that it is almost over.

Happy birthday?
How can we even say it?

Yet this decision, your decision, is a gift, of sorts.
And there are other gifts.

Loving life.
Coming back from the dead many times this past year to have more of it.
Coming out of this last coma five days ago.
Making it to ninety today, like you wanted.
The silver ring of nine hearts we had made to celebrate that long life.
The soft floral shawl that's warm and pretty, the only color in the room.
That great cup of coffee we brought you this morning.

It made you sigh happily as you sipped it.
I never thought it would be your last.

❀

But there are more gifts.

A long and happy life with Dad.
A wonderful doctor who tends your spirit.
Who tells you the truth about your body.

Your two girls, as you call us, daughters who protect your independence.
Who support your right to live – and now die – the way you want.

Being able to talk with us about anything, even this,
your plan to stop eating and drinking.

Having us honor your wishes.
The only gift we can really give you now.

I never thought wishing you Happy Birthday would break my heart.

Safe trip, you say to us when we leave your room tonight.
You too, Mom, I say softly in return.

93

❀

JUDITH
BARNES

FUNNY THING ABOUT DEATH

Death and taxes are mentioned together.
Death and humor?
Not so much.

Most people don't find death or dying funny.
But good humor does live there.

Day One, Morning
"I thought I'd take a little nap here."

Mom was lying on the dining room floor when we found her. And lying
through her teeth. But despite our dread, my sister and I couldn't
help but smile at her cheeky bluff. We knew she wanted to appear
healthy so she wouldn't lose her independence. What none of us knew
was that she would soon lose her life. And we couldn't have guessed
that laughter would become such good and welcome medicine.

Day One, Afternoon
"They're pains in the butt!" she muttered in the emergency room,
gesturing towards me and my sister. "That's why we're here, doctor,
to remove her pains in the butt," I said gravely. I got a chuckle
from Mom, a startled glance from the doctor and my sister.

Day Two
"If I can't live the way I want, I'll take myself out!"

Cancer was eating her alive but that tough-talking, movie-
mobster line shattered the grim expressions on the faces of
everyone around her bed and we all just grinned.

❊

GOOD TO
BE HERE

Day Ten
"We thought you'd want a nice lunch tray, dear,"

For over a week, Mom has refused to eat or drink, choosing her own death rather than the one cancer would force on her. Armed with all the legal papers necessary to support her wishes, I thought we were ready to deal with anything…except a lunch tray accidentally brought by an aide. I hesitated. "Mom?" I asked. "If it was lunch from Milano, I might think about it," she answered drily, referring to her favorite restaurant. "But it's hospital food. I'd rather die."

Day Fourteen
"I need to use more makeup," I told Mom when she returned to her room after tests. While napping on her empty bed, I had been mistaken for her: a dying, elderly woman. "At least more blush," she said.

Day Fifteen
"Sorry I'm late Mom, but I think I just got engaged."

Having gone for a walk in the medical center, I had innocently stumbled into a locked area for men with advanced dementia. A growing line of amorous elderly men had excitedly followed me around before all hell broke loose as I pushed open a door, setting off the alarm and the men.

Day Eighteen
After almost three weeks of not eating or drinking, Mom asked me in a small voice why it was taking so long for her to die. "I don't know, Mom," I answered, so sad I almost couldn't form the words.

Then before I could stop myself, "Maybe you're a vampire…you know… maybe we're dealing with the undead here." Horrified, I froze.

"Always loved that about you, that irony," she rasped with a laugh.

Day Twenty, Late at Night

Exhausted, I called the nursing desk to check on Mom's condition before going to bed. She was resting quietly but wasn't eating, the aide said.

I stammered out a shaky reply, hung up the phone and broke into helpless, hysterical laughter. Mom had been comatose for two days, on morphine around the clock and hadn't eaten for almost three weeks.

Resting quietly but not eating? I know you'd appreciate that irony, Mom.

Day Twenty One

Mom died just before dawn.

Driving to the funeral home in Vermont in the cold early morning light, I saw the pig. Sparkling in the weak sunlight, the big, fanciful, welded-steel pig has long stood by the side of the road in front of a barbeque place. Inside the pig is a smokestack that puffs out the rich, barbeque smoke and blows it across the road.

The pig was a family favorite, and the sight of it always made Mom hungry. "Best advertising in the world," she used to say.

Crying uncontrollably, I pull into the parking lot by the pig.
I open the window and inhale deeply over and over.
I want the smoke to reach up into the heavens and Mom.

Eat! I think, looking up.
Eat, Mom!
And let me hear you laugh.

❄

THANK YOU NOTES

You taught me to send thank you notes almost as soon as I could write.

When people are kind enough to give a gift, you told me, you need
to thank them promptly and tell them what the gift means to you.

At first I wrote the notes because you made me.
But as I grew up, I wrote them because I wanted to.

I enjoyed giving thanks for nice things or nice times, comforting thoughts
in tough times or just because somebody was part of my life.

That's why I'm writing this to you, Mom.

Oh, this thank you note is prompt, just days after your death.
The raw and awful newness of that death and the grim weeks
before it make this almost too painful to write.

But I will try.

First, thank you for not catching me one hot summer day
when I was nine and behaving badly.

You chased me around the dining room table and,
to escape your wrath, I fled to the bathroom and locked the door.
I'm pretty sure I lived to adulthood because of that near miss.

And thank you for the life you provided for me after I had been spared.

Even on days when you wanted to kill me – because of a stubborn
independence which I like to say only occasionally edged into
defiance – you always separated me from it. You let me know
that you loved me even if you loathed what I was doing.

❀

JUDITH
BARNES

That's a great gift, Mom, one I now try to give others.

Then there was your belief that I could do anything,
even when I didn't believe it myself.

That gift I gave you in return when you chose your own death,
rather than the one cancer had waiting for you: when you,
who so loved a good meal, chose to stop eating and drinking
after your 90th birthday lunch in the hospital.

During the unreal and unrelenting 21 days it would take you to die,
I supported your decision, sat with you and said yes when you asked
me if you were making progress, as you called it. Day after day, I
told you that you could do it, though it hurt me so to say it.

Your spirit prevailed even then.

No whining, you always said, and you never did. Not during
your lifetime, not during your agonizing death, when you surely
could have. As I write this, I look over at the NO WHINING
sign on my own desk, a reminder that I'm your daughter.

Thank you for the sense of humor we share, though we always
agreed yours was a more ladylike version of my own.

I saw that genetic link one very dark day towards the end.

Though frail and afraid, you were worried I had chosen not to
work for the weeks it might take you to die, as you put it.

❀

I tried to reassure you, telling you that my clients, who
over the years ...d also become my friends, were very supportive.

I added, with a dark grin, that being at the hospital every day had
even gotten me out of commitments I wished I hadn't made.

You grinned back weakly.

"A dying mother is a strong card to play," you rasped
in a small, dry, disappearing voice.

For that unflinching honesty, another trait we share, I thank you.

As I wrote in your obituary, that most public of thank you notes,
you were a truth teller whose great courage, spirit, grace and wit
helped you rise above the grim realities of those final weeks.

Finally, Mom, thank you for a lifetime of love and for the final
words my sister and I heard you say, "I love my girls."

99

❀

JUDITH
BARNES

ABOUT THE AUTHOR

© JOANN HOOSE

Judith Barnes, Ph.D., is an educator, entrepreneur, speaker and writer who likes doing new things, working with interesting people and being independent. So for 35 years she has had a national consultancy in communication. She was also a founding officer of a company commercializing micro fuel cells as a future power source, and has been active on behalf of civic, educational and arts organizations in her community. Her essays have been heard on public radio; she was co-writer and executive producer for a short film on personal responsibility screened at numerous film festivals (www.thecruxmovie.com) and featured on a public television program; and this is her first book. When not on a plane, she lives in Albany, NY with her cigar-loving cat.

101

❀

JUDITH
BARNES